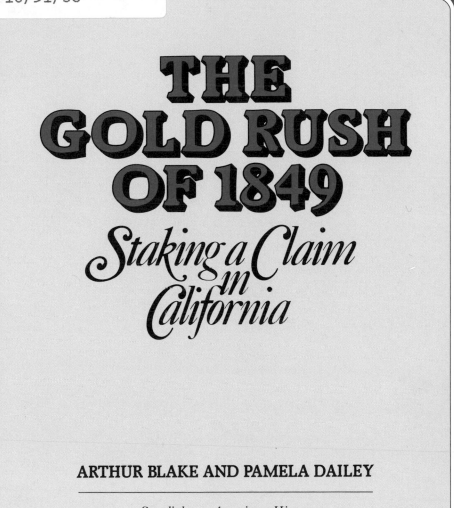

THE GOLD RUSH OF 1849

Staking a Claim in California

ARTHUR BLAKE AND PAMELA DAILEY

Spotlight on American History
The Millbrook Press • Brookfield, Connecticut

Cover photograph courtesy of National Museum of
American Art, Washington, D.C./Art Resource, NY
Photographs courtesy of California State Library: pp. 6, 30,
43, 44–45; North Wind Picture Archives: pp. 9, 27, 38, 41;
Historical Pictures/Stock Montage, Chicago: pp. 12 (top), 19;
Bettmann Archive: pp. 12 (bottom), 15, 22–23, 36; San Francisco
Public Library: pp. 16–17; New York Public Library Picture
Collection: p. 32; Wells Fargo Bank: pp. 35, 51 (courtesy Greg
Martin); Crocker Art Museum: p. 46; New York Public Library, p. 52.
Map by Joe Le Monnier.

Library of Congress Cataloging-in-Publication Data
Blake, Arthur.
The gold rush of 1849 : staking a claim in California
Arthur Blake and Pamela Dailey.
p.   cm.— (Spotlight on American history)
Includes bibliographical references and index.
Summary: The story of the California gold rush and its effect
on the character of the United States.
ISBN 1-56294-483-5
1. California—Gold discoveries—Juvenile literature.
2. California—History—1846–1850—Juvenile literature.
[1. California—Gold discoveries. 2. California—History—
1846–1850.] I. Dailey, Pamela. II. Title. III. Series.
F865.B63 1995 979.4′04—dc20 94-25773 CIP AC

Published by The Millbrook Press, Inc.
2 Old New Milford Road, Brookfield, Connecticut 06804

Contents

The Gold Rush
OF 1849

James Marshall in front of Sutter's Mill, where he found the gold nuggets that drew thousands of eager prospectors from all over the world.

1

GOLD!

The rivers run on golden beds,
O'er rocks of golden ore,
The valleys six feet deep are said
To hold a plenty more.

ON JANUARY 24, 1848, James Wilson Marshall, a carpenter from New Jersey, was 3,000 miles (4,800 kilometers) from home. He had been hired to build a sawmill where the American and Sacramento rivers joined near Coloma, California. As he walked along a ditch, he spied something gleaming at the bottom. When he picked it up and examined it, his heart began to beat faster. What he was holding in his hand looked like gold.

Marshall remembered that gold was soft. He bit into the nugget and saw that his teeth left marks. After flattening the piece with a hammer, he rode off to tell his employer. The mill belonged to a German immigrant named John Augustus Sutter, who had come to California in 1839, leaving behind a ruined business in Switzerland, as well as a wife and five children.

[7]

At that time, California was part of Mexico. When Sutter arrived, he applied for Mexican citizenship; a few years later the governor granted him nearly 50,000 acres (20,230 hectares) of land. It was on this land that he began to build his empire. His headquarters was a stockade known as Sutter's Fort, a place where wagon trains could rest and replenish their supplies. Before long, Sutter was managing orchards, livestock, a tannery, warehouses, and a flour mill.

By the time he hired James Marshall to build a sawmill on his land, John Sutter was already a wealthy man. Nothing, it seemed, could reverse his good fortune. Even when the United States declared war on Mexico in 1846 and claimed California for itself, Sutter remained unworried. He had always been a friend to Americans who moved to the Sacramento Valley, and he was sure that the United States government, in gratitude, would not interfere with his business.

What worried John Sutter was James Marshall's discovery. When Marshall dropped the flattened nuggets on his desk, shouting that he had found gold, Sutter felt a sense of dread. But first he had to make sure. He tested the nuggets by dropping them in boiling lye. They emerged unscathed. He then compared their weight under water with that of silver coins. All the tests indicated that the nuggets were indeed gold. Sutter now swore Marshall to secrecy, and they made a deal. If Marshall and his workers would keep quiet about it while building the sawmill, they could keep whatever gold they stumbled across.

But word, of course, leaked out. Too many people were finding gold nuggets in the Sacramento Valley. At first, stories of gold strikes were treated as tall tales without foundation. Within three months, however, just about everyone in California was a believer.

Monday 24th thisday
some kind of mettle was

177

was found in the tail race that
that looks like goald first discov
ered by James Martial, the Boss of the Mill.
Sunday 30 clean & has been
all the last week our metal
has been tride and prooves to
be Goald it is thought to be
rich we have pict up more than
a hundred dollars woth last
week

February. 1848
Sun 6th the wether has been clean

*An entry from the diary of a man named Bigler, one of the first
to make a profit from Marshall's discovery at Sutter's Mill.*

[9]

Eager to strike it rich, the citizens of San Francisco, Monterey, and San Jose dropped whatever they were doing and rushed to Sutter's mill. Fields were left untended; construction sites were abandoned; shops, offices, and even schools closed down.

In the spring of 1848, talk of gold was still confined to California, Oregon, and, somewhat later, to Mexico. The rest of the world went about its business undisturbed by golden dreams. The *New York Herald* got wind of what was happening near Sutter's Fort and published an article about the prospectors on August 19. But it was not until the governor of California sent samples of gold to Washington, D.C., in November that the discovery became national news.

On December 5, President James Polk made an official announcement to Congress, touching off the explosion that sent people from around the globe, from every walk of life, to seek their fortunes in California. Not everyone who made the long trip struck it rich. Some lost everything, including their lives; others barely scratched out a living. Together, however, these prospectors changed the face of the California Territory.

As for Sutter, he watched helplessly as people converged on his land. Ironically, he could not take advantage of the bonanza on his own doorstep. Because Mexico had lost the war, and the United States had not yet established a government in California, Sutter had no legal claim to his property. And once word of gold got out, his workers deserted him. Hordes of prospectors overran his land, destroying his crops, stealing his animals, and tearing up the earth with their picks and shovels. While others got rich, Sutter was financially ruined.

2

THEY CAME BY SEA

Like Argos of the ancient times
I'll leave this modern Greece;
I'm bound to California mines,
To find the golden fleece.

As RUMOR hardened into fact, gold fever spread across the country. Americans—who for generations had lived by a creed of thrift, hard work, and self-reliance—suddenly felt they could become rich overnight. After all, gold mining required neither an education nor special skills. A few tools, a way to get to the California hills, and a little luck were all you needed. As one woman whose husband went west wrote: "I am full of bright visions that never filled my mind before, because at the best of times I have never thought of much beyond a living, but now I feel confident of being well off."

Oh, the tales they heard, and the tales they told. Wherever people gathered in the winter of 1849, they talked of riverbeds lined with solid gold, of ravines chockablock with nuggets the size

One of the many guides to the goldfields, printed in Boston, 1849.

A cartoon showing the wild rush to reach California, by any means possible.

of a fist, of the farmer who carved out one thousand dollars a day with only a penknife and a skillet. Storytellers discovered they could stretch the truth and still be believed. One popular tale concerned the man who was found sitting on a 839-pound (381-kilogram) nugget. Refusing to budge, but desperate for something to eat, he offered $27,000 to anyone who would bring him a plate of pork and beans.

In 1849 the words "California gold" were on everybody's lips. But you didn't actually have to leave home to make easy money—not if you were shrewd and dishonest. Within months of the discovery at Sutter's Fort, thirty guidebooks to California appeared, most of them written by men who had never been there. New products suddenly hit the market. There was the "hydro-centrifugal Chrysolyte or California Gold Finder," not to mention the "Archimedes Gold Washing Machine," both advertised as indispensable to the successful miner. Gullible prospectors were also urged to ride the "aerial locomotive." For a mere $200 (payment in advance, of course) they could cross the country in only three days.

As most people with any common sense knew, though, the trip across the United States was long, arduous, and fraught with danger. The railroad that eventually connected the east and west coasts had not been built. There were not even any roads. Nevertheless some adventurous Americans had already gone west. Some of these pioneers had settled in the Oregon Territory, and the Mormons, members of a new religious group, had ended up in Utah. They had made the overland journey in wagons, a feat that was impossible during the winter. Still, many people could not wait for the spring. If not by land, they would go by sea.

The first sea route available to them was the traditional one taken by Yankee traders and whalers. Ships sailed to the southern tip of South America, where they might spend three months navigating the treacherous seas around Cape Horn. They then followed the Pacific coastline until they reached California. The trip covered 18,000 miles (28,800 kilometers) and took between four and eleven months, depending on the weather.

A faster but more expensive route was to sail as far as Chagres, a coastal village in Central America; next cross the narrow isthmus between North and South America; and then sail north from the old port of Panama City on the Pacific Coast. Today, ships can pass through the Panama Canal from the Atlantic to the Pacific Ocean in a matter of hours, but in 1849 crossing the strip of land between the two Americas was a difficult journey. First, travelers had to pay local boatmen to take them by canoe up the Chagres River. Then they paid guides to help them through the snake- and mosquito-infested jungle. For about six dollars they could ride in a clumsy two-wheeled oxcart; use of a mule or a horse cost a great deal more. Many simply walked—and died. The oppressive heat sapped their strength, and cholera, malaria, and yellow fever struck down thousands before they ever saw California. Would-be millionaires filled an entire cemetery in Panama City.

Those who survived the trip through the jungle then faced another obstacle. Not enough ships sailed between Panama City and San Francisco to handle the unexpected number of travelers. People often had to give ticket agents a huge bribe—sometimes as much as a thousand dollars—for a berth. Those who couldn't pay had to wait to book a passage at the normal price. Yet despite the expense and the risk, more than six thousand Americans took the Panama route in 1849 alone. A year later the number grew to twenty thousand.

In fact, within six months of President Polk's announcement, there was not a ticket available on any vessel leaving the eastern

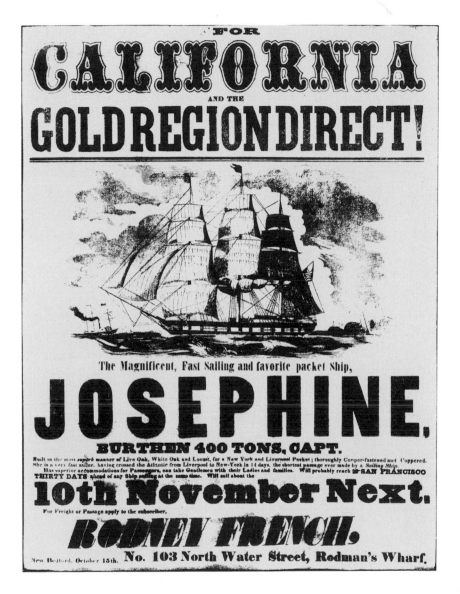

Travel by ship was expensive and dangerous, but in the winter of 1849 many people, in a frenzy to stake an early claim, responded to ads such as this one.

seaboard for parts south. All available ships considered seaworthy (and a few that were not) were called into service. Ships were so packed that passengers could barely move around; finding a comfortable spot to sleep was all but impossible. Hygiene was a problem, and diseases took their toll. Miraculously, none of the ships sank, and some 41,000 people arrived in California by sea in 1849. Of these, 25,000 were American, and all but about 800 were men.

By summer, about 400 deserted vessels lay at anchor in San

Francisco Bay, blocking the harbor. All their crews had jumped ship to join the passengers heading for the goldfields. To clear space around the docks, San Franciscans finally had to drag the boats ashore. Once on land, they were used as jails, warehouses, and shelters for a sprawling population of men and a few adventurous women. Almost overnight, the gold seekers had transformed a remote village into a rough-and-tough boom town where dreams of riches contrasted sharply with everyday squalor.

THEY CAME BY LAND

Oh, do you remember sweet Betsy from Pike
Who crossed the wide prairie with her lover Ike?
With two yoke of oxen, an ole yellow dog,
A tall Shanghai rooster and one spotted hog.

*T*HOSE WHO could not make the sea voyage stayed at home planning and preparing for the overland journey. Impatient prospectors feared that all the gold would be gone by the time they reached California. But they had to wait for warmer weather and the spring grass that would feed their livestock along the way. When the time finally came to leave, most people joined up with a "company," or wagon train. Each traveler paid a fee, usually about $200, to cover the costs of the wagons, animals, and supplies. This sum was as much as a half year's wages for many people, but it was worth it. Traveling in a group meant safety and companionship over the long months. Many of the men who struck out on their own died of thirst or starvation. Others experienced such hardship and loneliness that they went mad or committed suicide.

*Prospectors set off overland with picks and shovels and pans and with
provisions for the long, hazardous journey west to California.*

People who staked their futures on finding gold were known
as "Forty-Niners" or "Emigrants" or sometimes "Argonauts." (In
Greek myth, the Argonauts were those who sailed with Jason on
the *Argo* to look for the Golden Fleece.) One such Argonaut was
William Swain, who left his family to run the farm in New York
while he went west to improve their fortune. He took a steamboat

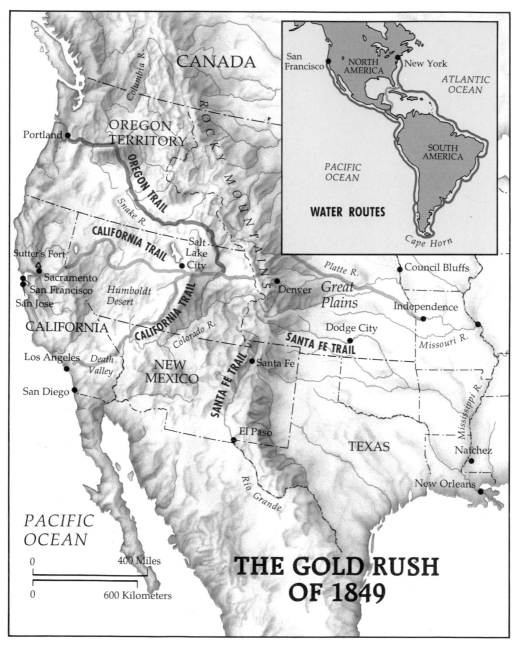

THE GOLD RUSH
OF 1849

CANADA

OREGON TERRITORY

Portland

ROCKY MOUNTAINS

Columbia R.

OREGON TRAIL

Snake R.

Salt Lake City

CALIFORNIA TRAIL

Sutter's Fort

Sacramento

San Francisco

San Jose

Humboldt Desert

CALIFORNIA

CALIFORNIA TRAIL

Denver

Great Plains

Platte R.

Council Bluffs

Independence

Missouri R.

Dodge City

SANTA FE TRAIL

Colorado R.

Los Angeles

Death Valley

NEW MEXICO

SANTA FE TRAIL

Santa Fe

San Diego

El Paso

TEXAS

Natchez

Mississippi R.

Rio Grande

New Orleans

PACIFIC OCEAN

0   400 Miles

0   600 Kilometers

WATER ROUTES

San Francisco

NORTH AMERICA

New York

ATLANTIC OCEAN

PACIFIC OCEAN

SOUTH AMERICA

Cape Horn

across the Great Lakes to Chicago, then continued down the Illinois and Missouri rivers to Independence, Missouri. It was in Independence, and in the towns of St. Joseph, Missouri, and Council Bluffs, Iowa, that most of the wagon trains began their westward journey.

Swain described his company of sixty-three members as "mostly smart and intelligent. There are among them two ministers and two doctors . . . also blacksmiths, carpenters, tailors, shoemakers, and many other mechanics. . . . We have eighteen wagons, fifty-four yoke of oxen, sixteen cows, and nine months' provisions. . . . We have rice, beans, flour and dried meal; two tons of bacon and 4,400 pounds of dried beef. . . . Mr. Bailey is a first-rate cook, and we live as well as at a tavern."

Like a great many others, William Swain set out for California with high hopes. On July 4, 1849, the *St. Joseph Gazette* reported that there were approximately 5,000 wagons (many with "California or Bust" lettered on their sides), 27,000 people, and 33,000 mules and oxen bound for California on that one day. So many wagons took to the road that summer that separate companies might be traveling only a few hundred yards apart. With their tall canvas tops rising above the high grass, the covered wagons resembled sailing ships, and so they were called "prairie schooners."

Although the Missouri towns marked for many travelers the last outpost of civilization, it was still nearly 2,000 miles (3,200 kilometers) to Sacramento. This was a daunting prospect. In his diary, Elisha Perkins of Marietta, Ohio, recorded these thoughts before leaving St. Joseph on May 20, 1849: "Henceforth we shall have no society, no sympathy for our troubles, & none of the comforts to which we have been accustomed. . . . So be it. Gold must be had & I for one am willing to brave almost anything in its acquisition."

Perkins and Swain and the other men, women, and children needed all the courage they could muster. Even at a fast clip, the journey from St. Louis to California took eighty-five days. Depending on the weather and the condition of the ground, a wagon

In the summer of '49, prairie schooners dotted the westward trails. It must have seemed that the entire country was in motion.

train covered between 5 and 30 miles (8 and 48 kilometers) a day. Many wagons started the trip together, but then as friendships formed or tempers grew short, people broke from the caravan, believing they could travel faster by themselves.

No matter how they made their way west, the Emigrants faced rough terrain, dust and wind storms, heavy rains and flash floods, buffalo stampedes, hostile Native Americans, wild animals, and rattlesnakes. Even mosquitos made their lives miserable. Near the border of the Platte River in Nebraska, Perkins recounted that his caravan was "most eaten up by mosquitos. . . . Never in my life did I have the misfortune to fall into the hands of such a pursuing merciless set."

The greatest threat to the travelers was disease. A cholera epidemic was raging through the Midwest at the time, and wagon trains carried the disease with them. People watched helplessly as their friends and relatives sickened and died. In that summer of 1849, more than five thousand corpses had to be hastily buried and left behind. Their shallow graves along the trail were a warning to those who followed of the hardships and dangers ahead.

To make the wagons lighter when the going got rough, many Forty-Niners threw out some of their belongings and provisions. Furniture, clothes, trunks, tools, and even salt, bacon, and flour were abandoned along the trail. Later, these same people, their food gone, were forced to beg from other Forty-Niners, not all of whom were ready to help. One traveler admitted that "it is hard to turn away a starving man 1,500 miles one way, and 300 miles the other, from any source of supply, but we are obliged to do it."

To avoid rough mountainous terrain, some caravans took the southern trails through El Paso, Santa Fe, or northern Mexico, contending with scorching deserts for most of the way. The majority, however, took the route that led north along the Platte River past Fort Laramie. They crossed the Rocky Mountains at South Pass, then descended to the Great Salt Lake, where they could rest and renew their supplies at the Mormon settlements.

The worst of the trip still lay ahead, though. Miles of dry, dusty land, offering little water or nourishment, had to be crossed before reaching the fertile grasslands of the Humboldt Sink. The Emigrants' joy on reaching this second oasis was short-lived as well. Just beyond stretched the Humboldt Desert, where the trail was marked with the skeletons of men and animals.

The final test before reaching the goldfields was the Sierra Nevada. Here the Forty-Niners had to navigate icy streams and narrow trails strewn with boulders. Even the descent was dangerous. It was so steep in places that the wagons had to be lowered with ropes. Adding to the travelers' discomfort was the fear that they could be trapped by early snowstorms in the mountains. This had happened to the notorious Donner party in 1846.

Every gold seeker knew the story. Eighty-nine men, women, and children crossing the mountains were only a day away from safety when an October blizzard blocked their path. They spent a terrible winter trapped in the pass with no supplies. After some members of the party died of cold and starvation, the others were forced to eat their bodies to stay alive. The grisly tale made headlines across the nation. A letter written by one of the children in the Donner party concluded with these words: "I have not wrote you half of the truble but I hav wrote you anuf to let you know what truble is." Her parting advice was remembered by wise Forty-Niners: "Never take no cutof's, and hury along as fast as you can."

CHILDREN ON THE TRAIL

DURING the first wave of the Gold Rush, most men left their families behind and headed west as part of all-male companies. But as time went by, more prospectors chose to bring women and children along. For the children the trip was an adventure; even their chores seemed exciting. They tended the animals, hunted for food, cooked, stood watch at night, cared for younger brothers and sisters, and scoured the prairie for the dried buffalo droppings, or "chips," used to fuel cooking fires.

Of course, children were not immune to the dangers of the journey. Many died of illness, drowned, or fell under the wagon wheels. Some lost one or even both parents to disease or accident and had to complete the journey alone. Travelers commonly told stories of finding children who had wandered off or who had survived alone after a tragedy had wiped out the rest of their family. Yet when hard times came, it was often the children who remained cheerful and kept everyone's hopes up.

*To children, the trip west was a thrilling,
sometimes dangerous, adventure.*

THEY CAME FROM EVERYWHERE

Oh, what was your name in the States?
Was it Thompson, or Johnson or Bates?
Did you murder your wife
And fly for your life?
Say, what was your name in the States?

WHEN THE Emigrants finally arrived in California, they were given yet another name. They were now called "Greenhorns," meaning people who were new to a place or situation. The Greenhorns included people of all nationalities, races, and backgrounds. They came from the South and the North, from England and France, Germany and Italy, from Hawaii and the Polynesian islands, from South America and Canada, from as nearby as the Oregon Territory and as far away as China. While the majority of the Forty-Niners came from the United States, it seemed as if every corner of the globe was represented.

Already in place were more than a hundred small tribes or clans of Native Americans as well as Californios, the Spanish-speaking Californians who had lived in the region for generations. When news of the discovery trickled south, Mexicans began to arrive, and then people from Chile, Argentina, and Peru. As word spread throughout the Pacific, the Kanakas, or natives of Hawaii (then known as the Sandwich Islands), began to pour in. From farther away came the Malaysians, who were often employed as sailors on Pacific trading ships. And after them came the first shipload of Australians.

Eventually, trading ships brought the news to China. A population explosion there in the early 1800s had almost doubled the number of people who needed food, farmland, and jobs. As Lu Ng, a laborer in Sacramento, recalled: "Crops had failed and floods had ruined our field. There was no wood left to cut in the hills. What else could I do?"

Many young men like Lu Ng decided to try their luck in the land they called "Golden Mountain." They had read the signs posted in their villages: "Laborers wanted for California in the United States of America. There is much work. Food and housing supplied. Wages are generous. There is no slavery. All is nice."

All, however, was not nice. More than any other people who took part in the Gold Rush, the Chinese suffered from discrimination. They were only allowed to work claims that had been abandoned by American miners, they could not become citizens or testify in court, and they were paid lower wages than other workers. Yet they put up with this ill treatment, and eventually some of them prospered. Many made their fortunes not in the California hills but by opening restaurants and laundries that offered the miners good food and clean clothing. Others worked for the companies that set up large mining operations in the mid-1850s.

People came to California not simply to look for gold. Many

Many Chinese joined the rush for gold in California, which they called Gam Saan, *or the Golden Mountain. They were met with low wages and prejudice.*

came to escape the oppression or poverty they endured in their homelands. The year 1848 was a harsh one in Europe: revolutions and economic depressions raged in many countries. France, in particular, suffered hard times, and people there were obsessed with news of the Gold Rush. The public's fascination with California gave the French government an idea. It sold raffle tickets for bars of gold and used the profits to send political enemies, gamblers, and criminals to California. But many honest French citizens also emigrated in search of a better life, and during the early years of the Gold Rush, 20 percent of the population of California was French. To the other miners they were the "Keskydees" because they were always asking *Qu'est-ce qu'il dit?* (French for "What's he saying?").

Another group of people that saw California as a fresh start were the Jews. Until the beginning of the nineteenth century, most Jews living in eastern Europe were confined to ghettos. When this restriction was lifted, many decided to leave and seek their fortunes elsewhere. California beckoned. Like the Chinese, many Jews set up businesses that served the miners' needs. They brought clothing, groceries, and other supplies from the cities to sell in the mining camps. One Jewish businessman imported canvas to sell as tents, but when he noticed how gold nuggets tore the miners' pockets, he took his needle and thread and whipped up a pair of sturdy canvas pants with double stitching. The man's name was Levi Strauss, and the pants he created are still known as Levi's.

What a sight all these different people must have made. To walk along a San Francisco street in the early days of 1849 was to see flannel shirts and heavy boots, frock coats and stovepipe hats, satin jackets and pigtails, serapes and sombreros, pantaloons and yarmulkes, and exotic Malaysian garb and tattoos. Black people, yellow people, white people, people of varying shades of brown, speaking dozens of languages, mingled and bartered with one another, all linked together by one common objective—GOLD.

Miners, wearing jeans, pan for gold in the Sierra Nevada.

5

SETTING UP CAMP

The site was bleak, the houses small,
The narrow streets unpaved and slanting,
But now it seems to me of all
The spots on earth the most enchanting.

THOSE WHO disembarked in San Francisco at the start of the Gold Rush were not prepared for what they found. Nor was San Francisco prepared for them. In 1848 the city was no more than a cluster of thirty or forty buildings. The Emigrants were also surprised to learn that the actual work of mining took place 100 miles (160 kilometers) inland. Obviously, the first order of business was to find somewhere to stay.

Because the few hotel rooms rented for more than most people could afford, miners hurriedly put up tents or flimsy shacks. These makeshift lodgings did little to protect them from the steady rains and the mud that covered the streets. The mud was so deep that carts, animals, and even people sometimes sank out of sight. Sanitation was nonexistent, and the city looked ugly and squalid in the daylight. At night, however, when thousands of whale-oil lamps burned and glowed beneath the slightly transparent tent cloths, San Francisco was transformed into a city of light.

Another unpleasant surprise for the prospectors was the high prices that local merchants charged for food and supplies. Eggs sold for $10 a dozen, flour cost $50 a barrel, a pick or shovel was $10, and two new shirts might come to $40. People who had run out of money began selling off their possessions.

When they were ready to travel again, the Forty-Niners made their way to Sacramento. There they heard rumors about recent strikes and rushed off to join the other miners. The camps they put up were often no more than temporary homes. Crude tents and shacks lined a trash-strewn dirt road or perched on steep hillsides overlooking the diggings. Their names—Grizzly Flat, Bogus Thunder, Cut Throat, Jackass Hill, Bladderville, Gouge Eye, Poker Flat, Tenderfoot Gulch, Shirttail Diggings, Mad Mule Gulch, Whiskey Bar, Git Up and Git—suggest what life was like for their inhabitants. Without wives or mothers to look after them, the young miners were hit hard by homesickness and disease; ten thousand died the first year.

They may not have looked like much, but the camps did try to create order. Since the gold territory was so remote, it was beyond the reach of the American legal system. The miners had to make and enforce their own rules. Each camp organized its own district, elected officers, and voted on a mining code. There were five hundred of these mining districts in California, and their codes regulated the size of the claim a miner could work and how he should mark it. In some very rich districts, prospectors had to be content with diggings of no more than 10 square feet (less than 1 square meter). The codes also protected miners from "claim jumpers," those who tried to take over the diggings of others.

A 1849 painting of miners' tents pitched on Telegraph Hill in San Francisco. The flag on top of the hill let people know that another ship was heading into the bay.

[35]

Next to a stream dotted with miners, recent arrivals dig a hole—"sink a pot." They will use the cradles to sift through the loosened dirt for gold.

That first year a spirit of equality existed in the camps. The miners, whatever their previous station in life, dressed the same, did the same work, suffered the same hardships, and enjoyed the same entertainment. Those who "put on airs" were quickly taught a lesson. When one elegant newcomer refused to socialize with his neighbors, they had him arrested and tried as a horse thief. It was a practical joke, but the snob got the point. If you lived in the camps, you were neither better nor worse than anyone else.

Unfortunately, within a year, this democratic attitude was challenged by some white American Emigrants who demanded the lion's share of power and profits. These so-called nativists felt that only Americans should be able to mine gold on United States land. In some districts rules were made barring foreigners—particularly Chinese and Mexicans—from staking claims. Nativists also imposed a tax of $20 a month on foreign miners and helped pass the 1852 Fugitive Slave Law and laws discriminating against the Chinese. Consequently, many non-American prospectors were forced to give up their claims. Some of them went home; others took jobs as laborers.

Panning for gold—filling a wash pan with gravel and water and then tipping the pan to let the water drain out— was a simple method that any beginner could master.

6

WORKING THE MINES

I'll take my wash bowl in my hand,
And thither wind my way,
To wash the gold from out the sand
In California!

THE HORDES of prospectors who descended on California had no idea of how much gold was waiting for them or of its exact location. The source was an underground vein of gold ore called the "Mother Lode." The vein was embedded in a quartz deposit a mile (1.6 kilometers) wide and 120 miles (193 kilometers) long. But the prospectors, unaware of the vein's existence, kept looking for "placer" gold—the dust, flakes, and small nuggets found in the dry gulches that had once been rivers.

Placer gold started out as part of the Mother Lode. Over the centuries, pieces of the rock containing gold ore washed down into streams where they mixed with sand and gravel. It was this layer of sediment that James Marshall had stirred up in digging out the stream for Sutter's lumber mill. Had he not decided to build the mill on this spot, who knows when or where gold might have been found in California.

One reason that the California Gold Rush attracted so many amateur miners was that placer mining was a simple and inexpensive process. All a miner really needed was a tool for digging and a wash pan. The first prospectors actually had even less. Working with pocket knives, they dug into rock crevices and then scooped out the gold with spoons. Others dug through the gravel at the bottom of dried-up riverbeds where gold was caught in pockets in the bedrock. The miners then "dry washed" this "pay dirt" by putting their "findings" on blankets and tossing them in the air. The lighter dirt blew away, but the heavier gold stayed in the blanket. Or most of it did.

Miners soon learned that they could save more of the precious metal with a washing pan. The method was brought to California in the summer of 1848 by Isaac Humphreys, an old mining hand from Georgia. Humphreys would fill his pan with gravel and then lower it into stream water. By carefully rotating the pan, and tilting it to let the water and dirt run off, he could pick out the larger stones. If there was gold, it remained in the bottom of the pan.

Even then the gold was not completely clean. It was scooped out and left to dry in the sun. Afterward, a gentle puff on the findings scattered the sand and dirt but left the heavier gold behind. The miners spent long days digging under the hot California sun or bent over and half-submerged in the icy water of the mountain streams. Men unused to such grueling labor sometimes collapsed, or gave up and went home.

The cradle, also introduced by Isaac Humphreys, was a more efficient device than the pan. A wooden box set on rockers, it had a perforated tray, or sieve, at the top, into which one miner shov-

The cradle was a faster and more certain way of separating water from dirt and gold.

eled gravel and another poured water. The larger rocks were trapped in this sieve, while the rest flowed down into the cradle below. A third miner rocked the cradle vigorously until the water washed the dirt out through an opening in the bottom. The heavier gold was caught by "cleats," or ridges, on the bottom of the rocker. Working together, miners could wash three or four times as much pay dirt with a rocker as with wash pans.

As time went on and the miners sharpened their skills, they dug more and more gold out of the land. At first, the average take was $20 a day, quite a lot of money when a common laborer earned only about $1 a day. At the height of the Gold Rush in 1852, 81,294,700 ounces of gold were mined. Yet because of the increasing number of miners, individual profits fell to $6 per day.

The miners now began to worry that there was not enough gold to go around. And what there was, they wanted quickly. They began to use the "Long Tom," a contraption something like a rocker but on a larger scale. By lengthening the cradle into a long wooden trough, the miners found they could wash even more soil. At first the troughs were only about 12 feet (3.7 meters) long, but the miners kept making them bigger until eventually some reached 100 feet (30 meters) or more. The day of the solitary miner with no more than a wash pan was just about over.

Some Forty-Niners formed partnerships to try river mining. They figured that riverbeds beneath flowing rivers contained gold just as the dried-up ones did. They built dams to divert the water so they could dig in the newly exposed river bottoms. Unfortunately, this method was not very productive. They never knew if, after weeks of work, they would hit pay dirt.

To reach pockets of gold buried in very deep bedrock, the miners developed a system called "coyoting." First they dug a main shaft large enough for the miners to climb through. Then they dug horizontal underground tunnels in all directions to locate the crevices in the bedrock that contained gold. It was exhausting and dangerous work, and miners could be crushed by cave-ins or overcome by the poisonous underground fumes sometimes found in mines. Nevertheless, coyoting was popular because it frequently paid off.

*These miners are using the Long Tom, a long version of
the cradle that required several miners to work together.*

In the winter, heavy rain or snow usually brought mining to a standstill. Prospectors who stayed in their cold, leaky cabins faced months of discomfort and boredom. Many preferred to pack up their bags of gold and head down to San Francisco, Sacramento, Sonora, or one of the other big towns for a bit of relaxation.

BLACK MINERS

THE GOLD RUSH was a once-in-a-lifetime opportunity for African Americans. Although slavery did not end until 1865, a number of African Americans had already obtained their freedom. In fact, among the first Forty-Niners to reach California were a number of black sailors off the whaling ships of New Bedford, Massachusetts. Used to foreign places and long voyages, they did well in the goldfields. When reports of their success appeared in the various antislavery journals back East, other blacks were encouraged to follow them.

And at first, most African Americans found life in the mining camps unthreatening. Mexican anti-slavery laws forbade the keeping of slaves, and when California became the thirty-first state in 1850, it was as a "free," not a slave, state. Although black miners worked with each other, they also formed partnerships with

prospectors of other ethnic groups. Photos from the time often show men of several races working claims together.

The fact that a slave had reached a free state did not automatically guarantee safety. In 1852 a pro-slavery group in California succeeded in passing the Fugitive Slave Act. According to this law, slave owners could legally recapture runaway slaves and force them to return to slave states. It was a law that could also harm a slave who had bought his freedom, as Stephen Hill learned to his dismay.

Stephen Hill was a former Arkansas slave who had accompanied his owner, Wood Tucker, to California. When Tucker found gold and returned to Arkansas, Hill stayed behind. He built himself a house and put in crops of wheat, barley, and vegetables. He also continued to work several mining claims.

Suddenly, a man named Owen Rozier appeared from Arkansas. Rozier said he represented Wood Tucker and ordered Hill to return to his owner. Although Hill maintained that he had bought his freedom and had the papers to prove it, he was arrested. Rozier then claimed Hill's property for Tucker. Hill's white friends were outraged and came to his rescue. They secretly harvested Hill's crops and sold off his animals and other possessions. When Hill was about to be sent back to Arkansas as a slave, they got Rozier drunk and managed to help their friend escape. Hill was last seen heading for Sonora. He had lost his farm, but he had money in his pockets and, more important, he still had his freedom.

Blacks and whites mine together in 1852.

"Sunday Morning in the Mines,"
by Charles Nahl.

7

REST AND RECREATION

Those were the days, no more are seen,
When all the girls loved me;
When I did dress in linen clean,
They washed and cooked for me.

BECAUSE THEY were working for themselves, the miners spent as many hours as they could digging for gold. They broke from work only when the weather was bad and at night and on Sundays. When not working, the men wanted to forget their aches and pains. They wanted to have fun. Even the smallest camp offered some kind of entertainment, usually a ramshackle cabin where the men could drink and gamble.

Miners who sought their fun in San Francisco could hardly believe their eyes. By 1850 the population had grown from eight hundred to thirty thousand. Saws whined and hammers rang out as buildings were erected at record speed. Many were prefabricated structures from China or Europe, shipped in pieces and put together by Chinese carpenters. Merchants around the world saw that they could sell anything to the newly rich miners. Basic necessities may have been missing, but cargo ships arrived regularly with every luxury, from French champagne and lobster to crystal chandeliers and ornate Victorian furniture. One rose fancier managed to import 15,000 plants representing 81 varieties.

As soon as the miners began striking it rich, gambling casinos sprang up everywhere. These establishments helped miners to relax; they also helped make them poor all over again. Gambling was a passion with the prospectors, whether the game was faro, poker, monte, euchre, dice, or roulette. Most carried their own well-worn deck of cards, known as the "California prayer book," and most promptly lost their savings to professional gamblers. Card sharks of both sexes were said to make more than $15,000 a month, and the casino owners probably felt that they had stumbled across the United States Treasury. Yet most miners accepted their losses cheerfully, believing there was always more gold to be found.

When they weren't playing, they were betting. They placed wagers on the bullfights run by the Mexicans, putting their money on the matador or on the bull. They bet on cock fights and dog fights; both were "sporting events" that went back centuries. During the wilder days of the Gold Rush, the miners trapped grizzly bears and pitted them against everything from bulls and donkeys to rats.

Most of these contests were gruesome and bloody, but occasionally they turned comical. At a fight between a bulldog and a wildcat, a miner recalled that "at the first kiss of the dog," the wildcat bounded into the orchestra and, turning a back handspring from the piano, landed on the contrabass, toppling "both player and instrument." The furious animal then plunged into the audience, causing everyone to run for cover. It was one of the shortest fights on record: 1 minute, 59 seconds.

The miners also looked forward to boxing and wrestling matches, which in those days were ferocious affairs, conducted almost without rules. Boxing matches were no more than fist fights that went on until one man didn't get up. Wrestlers employed moves like eye gouging and nose biting. Both sports were criticized in the press, and some people felt they should be illegal, but many miners clearly enjoyed such rough diversions.

There were also foot races on Sundays. Each contestant paid an entrance fee, sometimes as much as $100, and the winner took home the money. Side bets made the race even more exciting for the onlookers. Also popular were bowling and billiards. A hotel might do business with no private rooms and plumbing, but without a billiard table it had no chance of attracting guests. Bowling alleys could be found in almost every camp, and they were busy from dawn till dusk.

Forty-Niners who wanted to exercise their brains instead of their bodies played chess. The game eventually became so popular that many of the camps started chess clubs, and almost every newspaper published in the goldfields included a chess problem. Two of the clubs, in Eureka and Shasta, even played against each other by mail, their moves carried back and forth by the Wells Fargo stagecoach.

While there was no lack of games, something *was* missing—female companionship. More than 90 percent of the population in the camps was male, which made social life only a memory. Even when women started to come west in greater numbers, there was still only one for every six men. And the few women who came usually settled in the larger towns, not in the mining camps.

BAD MEN
OF THE GOLD RUSH

IN 1848 crime was almost unknown in California. Even in the camps, miners felt safe leaving bags of gold in their tents while they worked their claims. But once gamblers, con men, and dangerous criminals expecting easy pickings were lured to the area, and friction between the different races and nationalities grew more intense, crime became quite a problem.

San Francisco, especially, had its hands full. The police force was unable to control either the rowdy Forty-Niners or the real crooks. For months its citizens were terrorized by a gang of former U.S. soldiers called "The Hounds." These troublemakers usually harassed foreigners, especially South Americans. After a particularly vicious attack on one Chilean neighborhood, the public decided that The Hounds had gone too far. A committee of vigilantes arrested some members of the gang and sent the others packing.

Vigilantes also dealt with another San Francisco gang known as the Sydney Ducks. These exiled criminals from Australia specialized in setting fires in order to loot saloons and gambling casinos. In one eighteen-month period the city burned to the ground and had to be rebuilt six times.

The most famous outlaw of the Gold Rush was Joaquin Murrieta. So many stories were told about him that no one knows his true identity. In some tales, he had a ferocious sidekick who was named Three-fingered Jack. In others, his wife rode with him, disguised as a man. In all tales he figured as a Mexican Robin Hood—fearless, handsome, and generous to the poor.

Charles Nahl's painting of Joaquín Murrieta, about whom many tall tales were told.

Men took a much needed break from the hard, dirty work in the mining camps by engaging each other as partners in wild dances.

Still, the miners managed the best they could. There were parties and there was music, and when the dance band struck up a tune, half the miners pretended to be women. Dirty and bearded, the "women" wore patches on their clothes to separate them from the men; otherwise, how could anyone tell? In one camp, the miners had not seen a woman for so long that when an enterprising fellow put a lady's bonnet and boots on display, the homesick men willingly paid him $1 just to gaze at them.

The women who did come to California usually accompanied their husbands, although many were widowed along the way or after they arrived. Only the most adventurous came alone. Yet with or without a husband, a woman could make a good living. The miners needed a woman's touch. Their clothes were filthy and ragged, their bedding damp and moldy, and most lived on a diet of bread, beans, and bacon. A woman who did laundry or cooked was therefore assured full-time employment.

No matter what they did or how they looked, women were desired and sought after. "Women were scarce in those days," recalled Lucrezia Wilson, a boardinghouse owner. "I lived six months in Sacramento and saw only two. . . . Every man thought every woman in that day a beauty. Even I have had men come forty miles over the mountains just to look at me, and I never was called a handsome woman, in my best days, even by my most ardent admirers."

Recognizing an appreciative audience, female performers and actresses from all over the world came to California. Besides the nameless dance hall girls who entertained the miners in the fancier saloons, the Gold Rush attracted women with international reputations. Singers like Kate Hayes, the "Swan" of Ireland, and the American Ella Bruce were treated like goddesses and showered with bags of gold dust after each performance. The most famous was the sultry dancer Lola Montez, who remained in California for two years and whose "spider dance" was the talk of the camps.

Unfortunately, the more remote camps seldom got to see professional acts. They had to fall back on their own devices. The men put on variety shows in which miners recited poetry or famous speeches, or played their banjos, fiddles, or guitars. They performed plays in which men took the roles of women and children. And when they could, they persuaded Chinese jugglers and acrobats to perform. Being stuck in the middle of nowhere evidently didn't keep the miners from amusing themselves. In fact, it only made them more imaginative in their pursuit of entertainment.

8

CONCLUSION

For my heart is filled with grief and woe,
And oft do I repine
For the days of old, the days of gold,
The days of 'forty-nine.

IN THE MID-1850s the character of gold mining changed dramatically. The lone prospector with a knife or washing pan had given way to an industry that depended on cooperation among miners as well as on sophisticated equipment. The profitable mining camps turned into more permanent communities, while less successful camps became ghost towns. Those who resisted the new techniques wandered away, some to find gold in Nevada, Colorado, or Alaska. By the 1860s agriculture overtook mining as California's most important industry. Many of the Emigrants who never struck it rich in the gold mines remained to live and work in California. They turned to farming, planted orchards, opened shops, and began businesses, all of which fueled the state's growing economy.

The original inhabitants fared less well. At first the Native Americans had friendly relations with the other miners, but this changed as the number of Anglo-American Emigrants increased. White Forty-Niners would force the Native Americans off their land if they thought it contained gold. The tribes would then raid the mining camps for food and animals. The raids gave the whites the excuse they needed to massacre the Indians. Between 1848 and 1870, the Native American population in California fell from 150,000 to just 30,000. Some of the smaller tribes did not survive at all.

Gold mining also devastated the environment. Animals and birds were driven away, fish were killed by polluted streams, forests were cut down, and the ground itself was carved up. In their frenzied quest for gold, the miners had ravaged the once-beautiful California countryside.

But the cities prospered. Californians who had made fortunes in gold in one way or another began to show off their new wealth. In San Francisco they built lavish mansions, hotels, theaters, and gambling casinos and filled them with expensive furnishings and art. The old shantytown was no more. By 1870 San Francisco was the tenth largest city in America.

And in time women did come to California. As their numbers increased, so did their influence. Churches and synagogues were built, schools and libraries were established, literary and debating societies were founded. Eventually the transcontinental railroad was built, linking the east and west coasts. And so what began as a chaotic and sometimes barbaric period in the history of California in the end brought order and prosperity and secured the West as a vital part of the United States.

Chronology

1846	War between Mexico and the United States begins; U.S. forces occupy California.
1848	Mexico cedes California to the United States.
	On January 24, James Marshall discovers gold at Sutter's Mill, setting off a gold rush among residents of California. Soon the news reaches Hawaii, Oregon, and Mexico, and within a few months, it has spread to South America and across the Pacific to Asia and Australia.
	On December 5, President James Polk officially announces that gold has been discovered in California, and waves of prospectors from the eastern United States and Europe leave for California by sea.
1849	Wagon trains of Americans begin the long overland journey to the California hills in the spring.
1850	On September 9, California becomes the thirty-first state, entering the Union as a "free" state.
1852	Pro-slavery forces within California pass the Fugitive Slave Act, putting runaway slaves and even free African Americans at risk.
mid-1850s	Hydraulic mining methods are developed, allowing large companies to take over from independent prospectors.

Further Reading

Blumberg, Rhoda. *The Great American Gold Rush*. New York: Macmillan, 1989.

Lake, A. L. *Gold Fever*. Vero Beach, Florida: Rourke Corporation, 1990.

McNeer, May. *The California Gold Rush*. New York: Random House, 1987.

Van Steewyk, Elizabeth. *The California Gold Rush: West with the Forty-Niners*. New York: Franklin Watts, 1991.

Bibliography

Billington, Ray Allen. *The Far Western Frontier: 1830–1860*, ed. Henry Steele Commager and Richard B. Morris. New York: Harper & Brothers, 1956.

Christopher, Thomas. *In Search of Lost Roses*. New York: Summit, 1989.

Climo, Shirley. *City! San Francisco*. New York: Macmillan, 1990.

Daniels, Roger. *Asian America*. Seattle: University of Washington Press, 1988.

Davidson, Marshall B. *Life in America, Vol. 1*. Boston: Houghton Mifflin, in association with the Metropolitan Museum of Art, 1951.

Eisen, Jonathan, David Fine, and Kim Eisen, eds. *Unknown California*. New York: Collier Books, 1985.

Fisher, Vardis, and Opal Laurel Holmes. *Gold Rushes and Mining Camps of the Early American West*. Caldwell, Idaho: Caxton Printers, 1968.

Holliday, J. S. *The World Rushed In: The California Gold Rush Experience* (Diary of William Swain). New York: Simon and Schuster, 1981.

Jolly, John. *Gold Spring Diary: The Journal of John Jolly*, ed. Carlo M. De Ferrari. Sonora, Cal.: Tuolumne County Historical Society, 1966.

Lacour-Gayet, Robert. *Everyday Life in the United States*, trans. Mary Ilford. New York: Ungar, 1969.

Lapp, Rudolph M. *Blacks in Gold Rush California*. New Haven and London: Yale University Press, 1977.

Levinson, Robert E. *Jews in the California Gold Rush*. New York: KTAV Publishing; and Berkeley, Cal.: Commission for the Preservation of Pioneer Jewish Cemeteries and Landmarks of the Judah L. Magnes Memorial Museum, 1978.

Lewis, Oscar. *California Heritage*. New York: Thomas Y. Crowell, 1949.

Margo, Elisabeth. *Women of the Gold Rush*. New York: Indian Head Books, 1992.

McDougall, Walter A. *Let the Sea Make a Noise: A History of the North Pacific from Magellan to MacArthur*. New York: Basic Books, 1993.

McNeer, May. *The California Gold Rush*. New York: Random House, 1950.

Perkins, Elisha Douglass. *Gold Rush Diary: Being the Journal of Elisha Douglass Perkins on the Overland Trail in the Spring and Summer of 1849*, ed. Thomas D. Clark. Lexington: University of Kentucky Press, 1967.

West, Elliott. "Wagon Train Children." *American Heritage*, December 1985.

Index